Front through

ALL RIGHTS RESERVED
IN A RETRIEVAL SYS
PAINTINGS, OR TRANSM.   ..... . ᴏʀᴍ. ᴏʀ ʙʏ ANY MEANS (ELECTRONICALLY,
PHOTOCOPYING RECORDING, OR OTHERWISE) WITHOUT THE PRIOR WRITTEN PER-
MISSION OF THE PUBLISHER.

PRINTED AND BOUND IN THE UNITED STATES OF AMERICA

C & C Publisher Art Works
Charles Jones
1532 W FARGO 2S
P.O. Box 268153
Chicago, IL 60626-8153

U.S. $20.95 ISBN 0-9643501-3-0
Canada $30.95

Certification of Registration
This certificate issued under the seal of the Copyright Office in Accordance with title 17, United States Code, attest that registration have been made a part of the Copyright Office records, in particular Form VA, for a work of the Visual Arts, United States Copyright Office.

Copyright Office
Library of Congress
Washington, D.C. 20559

By Charles Jones © August 1996
REV: April 15, 2000

No patent liability is assumed with respect to the use of the information contained herein. Although every precaution has been taken in the preparation of this book, the author/publisher have used the best efforts in preparing this book and assume no responsibility for errors or omissions. Neither is any liability assumed for damages resulting from the use of the information contained herein. C & C Publisher Art Work, and the author make no representation or warranties and specifically disclaim and implied warranties of merchantability or fitness for any particular purpose and shall in no event be liable for any loss of profit or any other commercial damage, including, but not limited to special incidental, consequential, or other damages.

DEDICATION

Special dedication to my immediate family, far left Edward Jones, Cornelius Laughlin (Charles's son) Charles Jones, Willie Jones, Matthew Jones, Mother, Mary Ann Jones, Joseph Jones, bottom kneeling John Jones, Ethel Person and Zyrone Jones.

To my knowledge we only live once because that's all I know is one life therefore we might as well enjoy life while we can with the breath that takes us a little bit farther in life, taking in consideration that one day that last breath will leave us meaning death will occupy what is left of us.

TABLE OF CONTENTS

DEDICATION ....
TABLE OF CONTENTS III
PREFACE IV
ACKNOWLEDGEMENTS V
INTRODUCTION VI
BRUSHES 1
CHEMICALS 2
PAINTS 3
ART EXHIBITION 4
BOOK SIGNING 5
OPAQUE PROJECTOR 6
CHAPTER (1) SETUP CANVAS, EASEL 7
CHAPTER (2) SINGLE WASH 11
CHAPTER (3) CREATING PAINTING FROM PHOTO 27
CHAPTER (4) MULTIPLE WASH 30
CHAPTER (5) ADDING STORIES 66
CHAPTER (6) ILLUSTRATIONS NO STORIES 89
CHAPTER (7) PICTURES SCANNED & AIR BRUSHED 112
NOTES 134
INDEX .... 135 TO 137
ORDER FORM 138
COMMENTS 139, 140

PREFACE

This book is designed to show enthusiasts and artists the various forms of art such as the different styles in Oil Paintings, Free Style Paintings using your imagination, Computer techniques such as air brushing.

My whole purpose, it is to show the individual how to find within them self the true form of art, that can be seen today and in some cases ways. Creating portraits meant paints, I have tried to separate the difference between using an opaque projector and your own natural or developed skills. First of all using your own natural skills or gifted skills form trial and error, having the desire to do something, and trying to perfect it. To instance on page 43, 85 the painting called PLAYERS OF THE CITY 1973 was created from reading a poem. This called creative because from my opinion both creative and imaginary skills were used. There were no mechanical devices used in this painting and it was sketched by hand and I was relying on the information that I was reading.

However, on page 97 the painting PORTRAIT OF YOUNG MAN was constructed using an opaque projector because it was being done for a potential customer, and the opaque projector was used for accuracy making sure that the face of the person was matched as closely as possible to the photograph. Incidentally this was done from photographs which were placed inside the opaque projector and projected onto the canvas as you can see by looking at page 40, mixing the proper colors and then painting directly to the canvas or you succeed that this is a perfect idea paint all the shadows in, then continue with the other colors after it is set up.

Furthermore, there is another creative and visual painting on page 71 called KILLING OF A TWO-YEAR-OLD. This was done completely differently because this was an actual incident seen by the artist one night in the summer of 1993. I heard a gunshot fired looked out of the window and there lay a young victim from a pool of blood. A spectator was kneeling over the lifeless body. In this particular painting both mechanical devices and natural skills were used to recreate the incident. It was a lot of work done just to recreate the painting what I had to do was go out and find someone to help me put this incident back together. The use of a camera, phone, and the opaque projector were used then atmosphere was created using my imaginary thoughts on how the spirit of the child may live.

If you want to piece a portrait together or someone wants you to put another person with them standing together, then read page 82, 83, HUSBAND AND WIFE. In this particular painting I used a fall-out photograph and only the head of the other person that was from a black-and-white photo. I did not have a model and I had only seen the other person's skin tone color briefly, so I used a fashion model magazine for the tones. I took the head of the person and matched it onto the torso, then took the full-size photograph of the other person and matched it onto the torso and brought them together making it look as one. This called creative and imaginary. I also used the opaque projector to blow up the other picture because it was done from a very small photo.

You will notice that there are some pictures that look like a surrealist picture merged with an animal this is to done with the use of a computer attached to it was a scanner and a small camera. I used that with these photographs to represent this particular style of Mental Art form another way this could be done with the use of your natural artistic skills just by painting the subjects onto the other object.

ACKNOWLEDGEMENTS

John A. Allen, Manager, Visual and Performing Arts, Chicago Public Schools.

Earl Calloway, Chicago Defender, thanks to him for the article representing my artistic history.

To George Armstrong Elementary School, 2111 W. Estes Avenue, Chicago, IL for allowing their students to grasp some knowledge form one of my books.

To Sifu Lee Iera, thanks to him for all his support and his many contributions.

To Sifu Clinton (Silky), of the Green Dragon Society, for teaching and showing me, that hard work, exercise, training and sparring can help you spiritually mentally and physically,

Mr. John Norgard, Trico Graphics, Inc., Chicago. IL thanks to him for his advice on the four color processing toward one of my paintings and other opinions.

Ms. Barbara Archie, Chicago, IL thanks to her for her enthusiastic show of support and many contributions towards this book.

Henry L. Jones, thanks to him for his contributing to this book.

Thomas Pas of CHICAGO PUBLIC SCHOOL PRINTING DEPARTMENT STAFF, for their hard work and advise toward my first book.

Fred Hunter, CHICAGO PUBLIC SCHOOL for his assistance in editing a portion of this book.

Reese Nicols, of (DCFS) I thank him for permitting me to paint from one his photos. His journey to Africa made it possible.

INTRODUCTION OF AN ARTIST

My name is Charles Jones, I am an African American from the City of Chicago, and I am pleased to share with you a part of my life as an artist an artist and painter, born her on March 30, 1953.

I had a desire to draw from the day I had used crayons and pencils in elementary school. Later, in the upper grade center, I learned a little about blue print reading. As life went on, I learned more when I went to vocational schools, where I learned to paint in oils, watercolor and acrylic; pastels and chalk. I stayed with oils because they look longer to dry, which allowed me time to blend the colors.

While trying to gain some skills in art, I was suffering from a lack of adequate education and severe poverty. Simply because I was born of a darker color, I was kept in a dilemma with different races and origins. Therefore, I am writing this book in anticipation that some of the indigent people of color may be inspired by my work, an d that they will foster hope form it.

This book is basically designed to help African Americans understand a variety in black art known today, but in a primitive and civilized type of atmosphere. Some minorities, people of color, hopefully will come to admire, respect and understand these paintings that Illustrate present day artwork as seen and painted from some parts of the playgrounds, projects, and in the Chicago city streets. Some portraits portray the instant look of a race being genocide.

If you allow a person an education as a c... ... or educated and released from pri... but keep him or her from getting a job. W... good is the education if you are not going... profit from it? How can a person sustain ... without the necessity of having a job or so... other support. Yet while another race ha... the job market, then how can you hav... dream of hopes in living a decent life w... there are total discriminating circumstance... Some jobs pay so low that it will be con... ered a form of slavery, another form of ge... cide.

As to computer skills I have to thank Pat... Martin who have helped me with some of ... technical support in learning how to put ... parts together that make up t he compu... system and software that help make the ... operate properly.

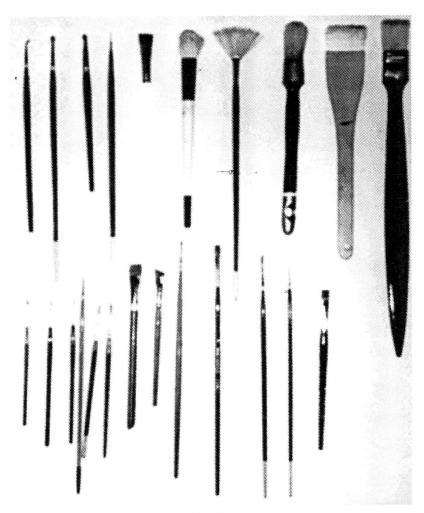

BRUSHES

Tools that you should be getting familiar with are your different types of brushes especially when you are painting portraits such as life-size type, meaning close to the actual size of the person's face using small brushes such as number 000,00, 1,2 round type of flat type number 0, 1, or 2 the bigger the brush the more area you want to cover as you can see in the following photo. Observe the brushes closely and you can see why you need smaller brushes for eyebrows, eyelashes, hair, details in the ear, and around the teeth etc.

CHEMICALS

Basically the chemicals that were used to mix these paints together were linseed Oil, Turpentine, Paint Thinner, Paint Medium, and Modeling Paste which was used only to show special effects, however, you must use some kind of palette knife; probably any kind will do. The palette knife is flexible and allows you to create different colors or blend colors together.

PAINTS

The types of paints used in this photo and all the paintings that I used were oil paints excepts for one which was done in acrylic. The following names of the paints used are Titanium White, Lamp Black, Cadmium Red Medium Hue, Indian Red, Burnt Orange, Quinarcridone, Yellow Ochre, Cadmium Yellow Medium Hue, Naples Yellow Hue, Raw Sienna, Mica Gold, Unbleached Titanium, Cadmium Yellow Light Hue, Sap Green, P:hthalo Blue, Monestrial Green, Cerulean Hue, Cobalt Blue Hue, Raw Sienna, Raw Umber, Burnt Sienna, Burnt Umber, Cerulean Blue Hue, Prussian Blue, Cobalt Violet Hue, Cadmium Red Medium Hue, Terre Verde.

ART EXHIBITION IN CHICAGO HEIGHTS
AT VERONICA ALEXANDER'S HOUSE JUNE 197-

To Veronica Alexander — thank her for allowing me an opportunity to setup a private art show at your house. It was an inspiration to have one of my books and artworks distributed in your town. Hopefully it will shed some light upon enthusiasts and victims in society and achieve my dream once goal.

CHARLES JONES
book signing and art exhibition

Seen here at the BLACK LIGHT FELLOWSHIP bok store on Chicago's West Side June 24, 1995. Photo by Herney L. Jones

USING THE OPAQUE PROJECTOR

You can use this machine to help you blow up or project the picture on to a canvas and paint the subject directly to the surface allowing an accurate drawing.

CHAPTER (1)

Setting up illustrations on canvas using brush, paints, easel in the sitting position hsown in the following pages.

Illustration by Charles Jones

(1)

Setting up your c
starting your points
sure you have a
easel, and the type o
and other materials
for painting

Observe the other p
these illustrations, y
Chapter 2 for furthe
terms

(2)

Creating, there are
that can be bough
you can get many at
store, such as BLA
and Drafting supp
the range starts at
canvas to stretch can
ally with cotton
prime canvas w
already attached
pieces of wood, wh
the back that folds
er. Observe the p
the photo it was
something like wh
painting on without
line on it.

You can get an inexpensive easel for about $19.00 and up depending on how much money you want to spend. The easel would look something like what I am painting on. The canvas sits on a piece of wood that supports it and can be adjusted lower or higher.

You can observe more of this painting on this particular picture, by going to Charpter 2 single wash (see page 14)

(5) Try to make yougself as comfortable as possible when you are painting and concentrate on your subject.

CHAPTER 2 SINGLE WASH

Explaining and demonstrating the single wash using linseed oil mixed with turpentine.

CREATING THE WASH

USING RAW UMBER OR BURNT UMBER MIXED WITH TURPENTINE IN THE FOLLOWING SIMPLE PROCEDURES.

PRACTICING THIS TECHNIQUE WILL ALLOW YOU TO CREATE A BETTER PAINTING WHEN YOU START APPLYING OTHER COLORS OVER THE BURNT UMBER OVER THE WASH.

I WILL GUIDE YOU THROUGH THESE STEPS BY EXPLAINING EACH ILLUSTRATION AS SHOWN.

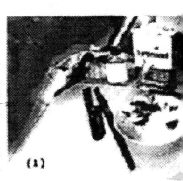

(1)

Picture (1) shows the plate, a tube of paint which is burnt umber, now small portion of this paint pushed out of the tube onto the plate. Behind the plate is the can of turpentine next to that is the linseed oil. Left of a number 5 brush, palette knife and an old rag or towel. These are items that I used to start a painting or subject.

Examples (2) pour some linseed oil into the plate with the burnt umber

Examples (3) pour some turpentine into the plate with the linseed oil

Examples (4) mix these two chemicals together and then add the burnt umber in small portions using the palette knife this will create the wash

Examples (5) take the number 5 brush and let part of the wash get on brush then start adding this to the subject all ways add this to the shaded of the subject first because later you would be adding other colors over wash.

Examples (6) start applying this wash to the subject only to the shaded area for now.

The rag is to keep excessive paints off the canvas and brush. The other pages following these illustrations will give a good idea how to start your painting.

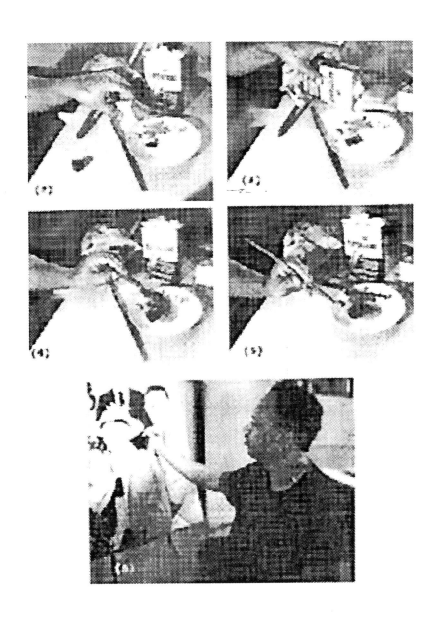

SARAH GARDNER'S FAMILY
40X 30 OIL PAINT

TEN YEARS APART SHOWING GROWTH FROM YOUTH TO MAN

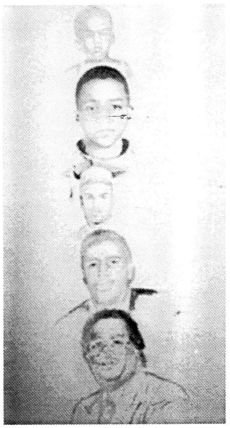

22X30 oil paint. This painting representing the growth of a young man from child hood to adulthood. As you can see starting from the early juvenile to young boy, young teen, young adult and progress to older adult. I used burnt sienna mixed with fast drying linseed oil and turpentine to start this painting off then let dry. I applied modeling paste to show special affects, so that I could later apply the burnt sienna on top of this modeling paste. After letting dry, referring to the background, I used zinc white with light blue and fast drying linseed oil. I then applied naples yellow and zinc white to each subjects face letting it get tacky then applied raw sienna and for shadowing used burnt umber then lastly used black for some detailing and to show contrast.

INTERMEDIATE FAMILY MEMBERS
30X30

"Intermediate family members "30x30 oil paint. Using fast drying linseed oil mixed with burnt sienna high lighted each subject let dry then applied raw sienna mixed with linseed oil, let dry, later used naples yellow mixed with linseed oil and a small portion of white let dry, continue to use raw sienna in three separate coats then used small portions of burnt sienna mixed with linseed oil. Whatever the subject's colors are try to mix these colors matching them as close to what you are seeing, and then finished with raw umber for shadows and details. Before the background was completed, I used modeling paste to create a different type of look. Unlike the other unfinished paintings of intermediate family members" was created using five photos, then each was painted separately, to look as if one complete family portrait

PORTRAIT OF LISA MCDONALD'S BROTHER AND WIFE
18X24 OIL PAINT CANVAS

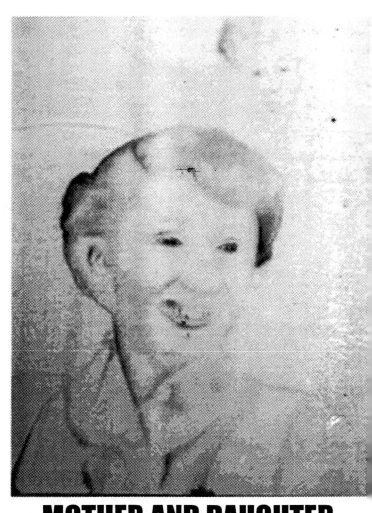

MOTHER AND DAUGHTER
18X24 OIL PAINT

A LAMBERT OF AFFIRMATIVE ACTION
18X24 OIL PAINT

THE ADMIRER OF AFRICAN AMERICAN LEADERS.

MARRIED COUPLE EMPLOYEES OF D.C.F.S. WORKERS

18x24 Oil Paint, Unfinished

PRIMITIVE INDIAN WOMAN

(1)

PRIMITIVE INDIAN WOMAN
24X36 OIL PAINT ON STRETCH CANVAS

SKETCHED OUT USING BURNT SIENNA AND MIXED W LINSEED OIL AND TURPENTIE.

SEE STEP (1) PAINTING NOT FINISHED, BUT AT A LATER D/

HOMELESS PERSON SLEEPING IN THE LOWER WACKER DRIVE UNDERGROUND-PAINTED IN OIL LOCATED IN CHICAGO IL -1993

PORTRAIT OF VERONICA ALEXANDER
18X24 OIL AUGUST 12, 1994

MARTIAL ARTS EMBLEM 18X24 OIL

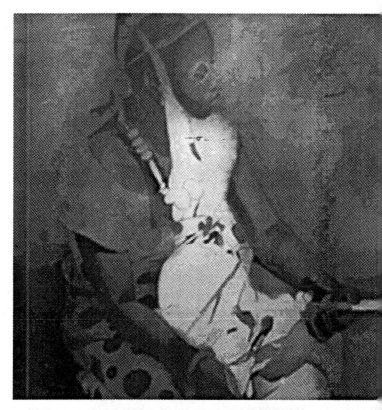

AFRICAN WOMAN MAKING INSTRUMENT
36x36 Oil paint May 15, 1995
Burnt sienna mixed with linseed oil and turpentine.

CHAPTER [3]

CREATING A PAINTING FROM PHOTOS

You can create a painting from the following photos and create any background for it.

CHICAGO LAKE FRONT FAR NORTH SIDE

HOMELINESS MAN LIVING ON THE STREETS OF CHICAGO LOCATION 4500 N BROAWAY ON JUNE 25, 1996

CHILDREN AND PLAYING ON CHICAGO CABRINI GREEN PLAY GOUNDS JUNE 25, 1996

CHAPTER 4

SHOWN IN THE FOLLOWING PAGES ARE STEPS USING THE MULTIPLE WASH TECHNIQUE.

ON EACH PAGE ARE NUMBERED PAINTINGS. THE PHOTOS SHOW HOW I STARTED THROUGH COMPLETION. I THOUGHT THAT IT WOULD BE BETTER TO SHOW SEVERAL OF THESE ILLUSTRATIONS. THE INDIVIDUAL SHOULD UNDERSTAND THESE 36 PAGES OF ILLUSTRATIONS.

MICHAEL JORDAN, SLAM DUNK SHOT
22X30 OIL JANUARY 12, 1994

Completed with burnt sienna for shadow mixed with linseed oil as a wash, used raw sienna, burnt sienna, light red, zinc white, black mixed with zinc white for background.

MICHAEL JORDAN, SLAM DUNK SHOT

PORTRAIT OF THREE
OIL ON CANVAS 18 X 24

From start to finish raw umber oil paint was used; as the portrait progressed, additional colors were added, such as, naples yellow, raw sienna, cobalt blue, black and cadmium red.

Observe the three portrait on the following page.

These four examples can be understoo[d]
from reading the prior pages up to pages 5[...]

COUSIN AND BOYFRIEND
OIL PAINT, 22X28 APRIL 1993

THE FIRST PICTURE SHOWS WHERE I PLACED THE RAW UMBER PAINT, USING A MIXTURE OF LINSEED OIL AND TURPENTINE TO SET UP THE SHADOWS.

THESE SAME COLORS WERE ALSO USED FOR THE BACKGROUND.

PICTURES TWO AND THREE SHOW THE ADDED NAPLES YELLOW, RAW UMBER, BURNT SIENNA, AND RAW SIENNA, ALL IN LAYERS.

A PHOTOGRAPH DEVELOPTING INTO
AN OIL PAINTING

IN THIS PICTURE THE ARTIST HAS RECAPTURED THE LIKENESS OF A POORLY PRESERVED PHOTO.

PICTURE # 1 ON AN 18X24 STRETCHED CANVAS, BURNT UMBER AND RED, LIGHT BLUES OIL PAINTS WERE USED TO CREATE THE SHADOWS. THIS COAT OF PAINT MUST DRY BEFORE THE NEXT COAT IS APPLIED.

PICTURE #3. CONTINUING WITH THE SAME COLOR MIXTURE PROCESS AND ADDING MORE BLUE COLOR TO GIVE THE SHADOWS MORE DEFINITIONS. BLUE OIL PAINT IS ALSO USED FOR THE YOUNG BOY'S JACKET AND BOW TIE. CADMIUM RED FOR THE YOUNG GIRLS' JUMPER.

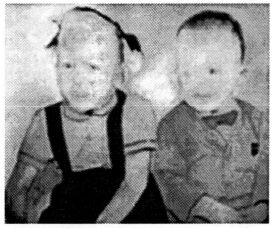

GIRLFRIEND - BOYFRIEND
18X24 OIL PAINT ON CANVAS, 1993

Used oil paint colors such as naples yellow, burnt sienna, raw sienna, raw umber, black, white, indian red and mica gold, for skin tone or shading also used camium yellow and white was used for background.

Picture # 1 raw umber and the other colors were used forst in setting to create a lightness in the dark areas, and as a guide in using light clors over darker ones. to do this, mix linseed oil and turpentine with raw umber until the consistency is very thin, to simulate a transparencyu. The linseed oil and turpentine will allow this paint to dry quickly.

In picture 2. a mixture of naples yellow and zinc white with linseed oil and turpentine was applied to the subjects face, legs, arms, etc.

In picture 3, continue using these colors until you begin the use of the heavier coats of paint which were used for definition.

In picture 4, using more of the same oil paints, the painting is completed after a desired frame is chosen.

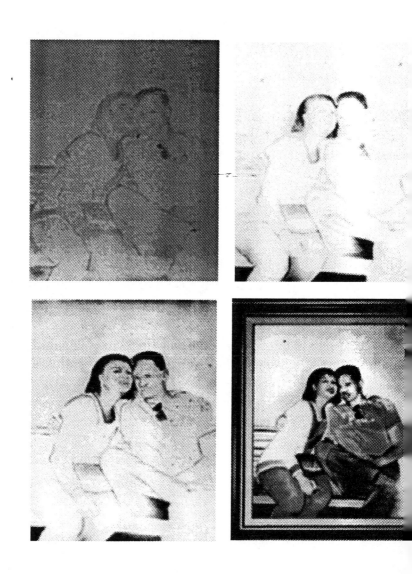

SELF PORTRAIT OF ARTIST AND SON
18X24 OIL PAINT APRIL 7, 1993

In picture 1, begin with burned umber to bring out shadows. In picture 2 start adding naples yellow, and raw sienna. in picture 3 add cobalt blue and phthalo blue to background.

Used same technique as above, but naples yellow was added with mica gold for a lighter tone.

Some of these picture may appear awkward, this is because i had to stretch them using a computer to create the same size photos.

REPEATED VIOLENCE

30X30 OIL PAINT ON CANVAS
JUNE 20, 1993

Repeated Violence" this painting was inspired because of an in incident witnessed by the artist one evening form an apartmeent window in public housing.

A group of teenagers were attacked by another group while playing basketball and were physically abused with pipes, etc.

REPEATED VIOLENCE

30 x 30 Oil On canvas

(1) (2)

(3) (4)

THREE GENERATION OF MOTHERS
18X24 OIL PAINT MAY 7, 1993

Portrait of three generations from grandmother to mother to daughter. completed in oil paint 18x24 final with frame.

Step one 1 brushed in oil paint layout with raw umber to set up likeness, shadows and shaded using mixture of linseed oil and turpentine. Step two 2 added more colors using burnt sienna. raw sienna, naples yellow, mica gold for skin tone and other colors for dress material including background.

THREE GENERATIONS OF MOTHERS
18 x 24 Oil Paint May 7, 1993

Portrait of three generations from grandmother to mother and daughter done in oil paint 18 x 24 final finish with frame.

Step one (1) head brushed in oil paint layout with raw umber to set up like shadows and shaded using mixture of linseed oil and turpentine. Step two (2) added more colors using burnt sienna, raw sienna, naples yellow, mica gold, skin tone and other colors for dress material, including background.

PORTRAIT OF MOTHER AND CHILD
30X40 OIL PAINT SEPTEMBER 1993

IN THIS PICTURE, PORTRAIT OF MOTHER AND CHILD THREE PHOTOGRAHS WERE TAKEN, THEN PUT TOGETHER ON A 30x40 STRETCHED CANVAS.

IN PICTURE# ONE, USING BURNT UMBER, OUTLINING THE SHADOWS CREATING THE LIKENESS.
PICTURE # TWO, ADDING MORE COLORING USING, WHITE, AND BLUE TO THE BACKGROUND.

PICTURE THREE SHOWS THE ADDITION OR MORE BLUE TO CREATE BACKGROUND, ASLO ADDING RED AND ORANGE AND SOME BLUE TO CLOTHING.

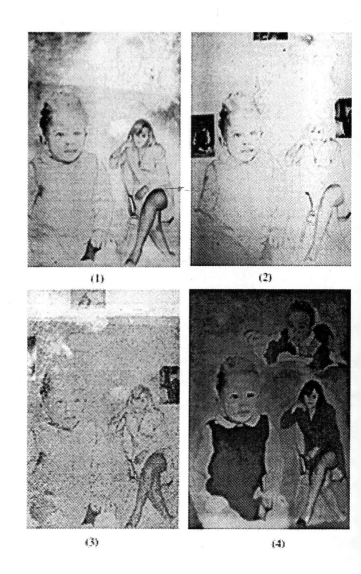

(1)　　　　　　　　(2)

(3)　　　　　　　　(4)

PORTRAIT
THE GRAY WEDDING

18X24 OIL PAINT ON CANVAS

Step one, shows the burnt umber applied using a number 4 and 2 round sable brush.

Step two, adding zinc white to the dress, mint green to the flowers, adding more raw umber to the tuxedo.

Step three, adding more zinc white to the dress and mint green to with a touch of cobalt blue mixed with some raw umber with ivory black for the tuxedo and mint green and zinc white to the background.

PORTRAIT
THE GRAY WEDDING
18X24 OIL PAINT ON CANVAS

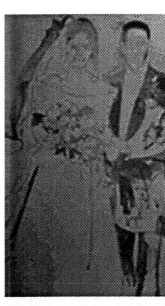

CHILDREN PLAYING ON C.H.A. GROUNDS
36X36 OIL PAINT ON CANVAS

Paints used to complete this picture were raw umber, raw siena blue black, red cadmium, yellow cadmium, zinc white, coblat blue, zap green and yellow orchard mixed with flesh including linseed oil and turpentin.

Step 1 ujsed raw umber mixed with turpentine linseed oil was used to cover the entire sketch known as a wash.

Step 2 showing here the painting that was actually reproduced using the photograph as a guide now created the oil painting.

In step 4 you can compare this photograph with the painting you have just produce.

CHILDREN PLAYING ON C.H.A GROUNDS
36 X 36 OIL PAINT ON CANVAS

Another one of my interesting subjects was three small girls gather underneath a playpen, above a small boy walks through the opening as they played.

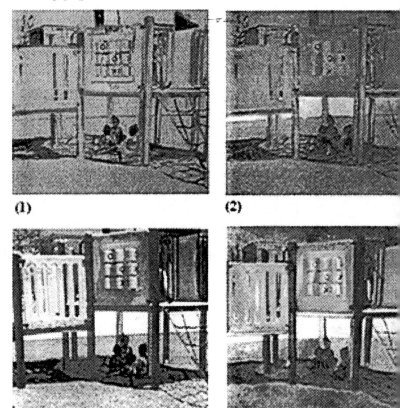

CHILDREN PLAYING ON C.H.A. GROUNDS

WOMAN CARING FOR A DISABLED WOMAN IN WHEELCHAIR
24X36 OIL PAINT ON CANVAS

I thought this painting would be an interesting subject. The female nurse caring for a disabled woman form a nearby nursing home takes a stroll in the park. The disabled woman is enjoying some sun and breeze.

It seems that the picture itself tells a lot more than a person being pushed through the park, in a wheel chair. It leaves more to the imagination than one can imagine.

Step (1) here in this painting I used raw sienna to sketch out the subject.

Step (2) I used more raw sienna, cadmium yellow, cobalt blue, zap green, and zinc white.

The final step in the painting shows where I used more of the same paints as in the other painting. Except that I added some ivory.

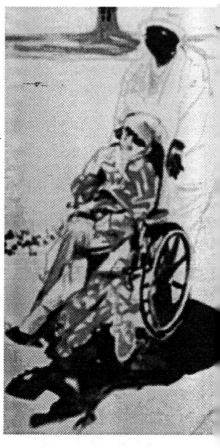

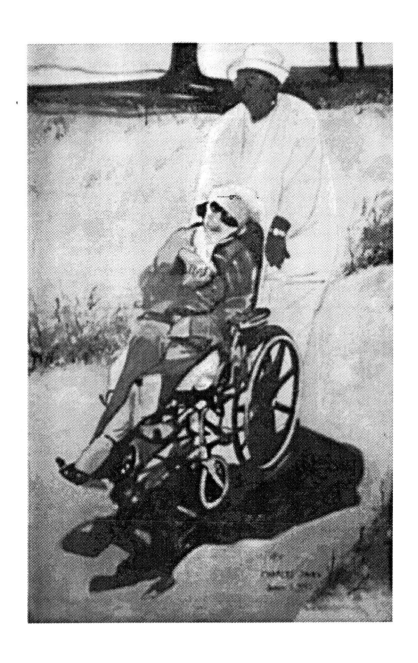

WOMAN CARING FOR A DISABLED WOMAN IN WHEELCHAIR

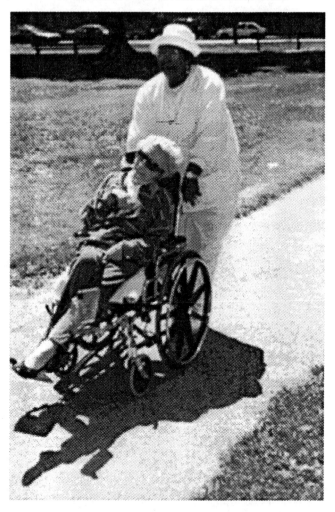

HANDICAPPED MAN LEADING A BLIND MAN

Another interesting subject was a handicapped man in a wheelchair going through a flea market as he lead a blind man they stopped and rested. the blind man had a plastic milk crate, which he use as a chair to sit on; he has a empty cup extended for passersby to make contributions. the man in the wheelcahir watched carefully, so no one takes any spare change from their precious cup.

Step (1), I used raw sienna, burnt sienna, cadmium red, zinch white and blue balck.
Step (2), the is finished this was recreated by using the a photograph which is shown in.
Step (3), is the phoograph, however, it was air brushed after the background was taken out.

ARTIST FANTASY OF BEING KIN
32 X 46 OIL, MARCH 5, 1995

STEP (1), USING A MIXTURE OF LINSEED OIL A TURPENTINE TO GET THESE AFFECTS.

STEP (2), USING LINSEED OIL WITH MIXTURE OF T PENTINE AND ADDING COBALT, RAW SIENNA, BUR SIENNA.

STEP (3), USING RAW SIENNA, BURNT SIENNA, R YELLOW, ORANGE, BLUE AND ZINC WHITE.

STEP (4), THIS PAINTING IS FINISHED, COLORS US WERE ZINC WHITE, COBALT BLUE, REDS, ORAN NAPLES YELLOW, GREEN MIXED WITH LINSEED AND TURPENTINE.

STEP (5), APPLYING FINAL COLORS DEPENDING YOUR ON DECISION.

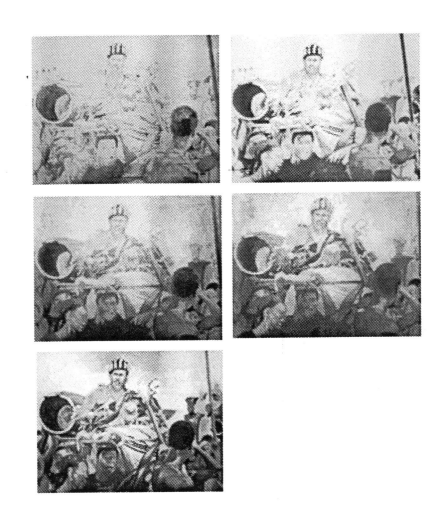

ARTIST AND WOMAN BODY BUILDING
24X36 OIL PAINT ON CANVAS

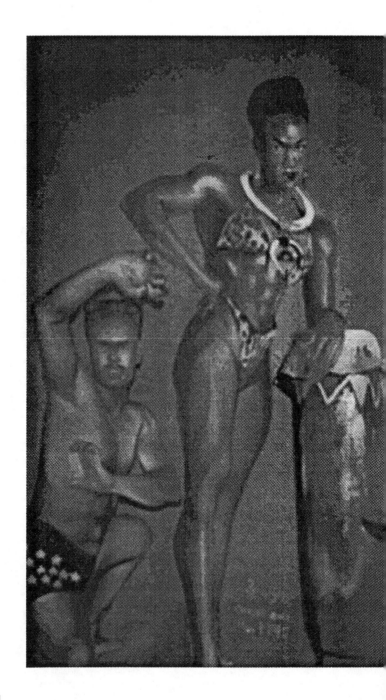

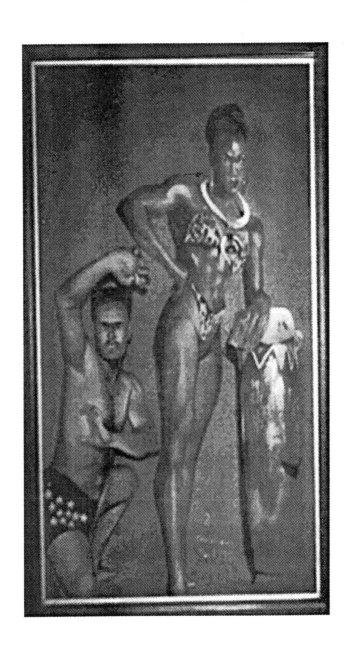

CHAPTER 5
adding a story to your painting

ADDING THE STORY TO YOUR ART WORK

Knowning that you can add a story to your art work or to an incidnent that you have seen, will make the picture or painting much more interesting.

See the foloowing pages along with the stores.

AUTOBIOGRAPHY OF THE PAINTING AFRICAN AMERICANS STRUGGLE TO SUCCESS FROM POVERTY

By Charles Jones

This painting represents the artist, Charles Jones and his struggle to become a good artist in art dealing with oil paints and what he felt while painting this picture.

The first three people, Malcom X, Harold Washington, and Dr. Martin Luther King, Jr. featured at the top of this painting on this 30x40 stretch canvas represent individuals trying to make a better life in a Caucasian atmosphere for African American people. Unfortunately, some of them lost their life at an early age but not in vain if their sacrifice fosters a better life for generations to come.

The middle of this painting represents great sports and politicians for instance Mohammed Ali, well-known for his three time victory Heavyweight World Boxing Champ, represents strenght and self advertisement. The female is Carol Moseley Braun, the first Black woman to become a U.S. Senator. She shows that African-American women can possess great leadership, Micheal Jordan represents a good role model for children. He shows that we are capable of leading our own to great success in sports and in school. The lighting coming from his fingers and his legs will help stiumulate and motivate us in seeing reality.

The last hree of the nine represent the homeless, the artist, and his loving son, cornelius P. Laughlin. The struggle to develop a healthy relationship with his son, and to help him shed some light on his future goals, and be careful not to fall victim to homelessness like some of us have.

We see sleeping in the alleys and other parts of the, or in abandoned buildings. however, many homeless victims became homeless due to unforseen circumstances such as drugs, poor family relationslhip, and economic pressure.

great leadership, Micheal Jordan represents a role model for children. He shows that w capable of leading our own to great succe sports and in school. The lighting coming fro fingers and his legs will help stiumulate and vate us in seeing reality.

The last hree of the nine represent the hom the artist, and his loving son, cornelius P. Lau The struggle to develop a healthy relationshi his son, and to help him shed some light c future goals, and be careful not to fall vic homelessness like some of us have.

We see sleeping in the alleys and other parts c or in abandoned buldings. however, many l less victims became homeless due to unfc circumstances such as drugs, poor family rel slhip, and economic pressure.

MOTHER PULLING BABY BOY ON TOY TRAIN

39 3/4 X 34 OIL PAINT, AUGUST 21, 1994. This painting was created as an example to show a mother who is also a drug user. Mother and child appear to be doing fine, howev mother is having problkems trying to eliminate her drug rel ed problems, and at the same time trying to establish a heal relationship with her son.

MY YOUTH, MY PAST, MY UNBORN, AND MY SON.

The artist visualizes his past with his ex-commonlaw wife with his unborn son, cornelius Pierre Laughlin, and his mother connie F. Laughlin and again after the baby is born she is seen holding him at about age four to six months old. The son appears again in the background at the age of ten years old. The old. The other boy standing in front of him is the artst himself at the age of ten yeras old who is the faterh of the boy in the backgouund and then the artist is also seen again sitting down in front of his ex-common law wife who is standing behind the artistl The artist in this apinting is apporoximately 28 hears old an upon completing this painting the artist is forty ears old.

Special technique used for background were modeling paste, palette knife for special features for a protruding effect, used zinc white mixed with light red, Indian red, for subjects skin tone used naples yellow, raw sienna, burnt sienna, burnt umber, burnt umber mixed with balck for the clothing used zinc white, orange mixed with yellow, bue hue, burnt sienna, green and blue back.

AN AFRICAN-AMERICAN MAN

30 X 30 OIL MARCH 30, 1994

This painting represents the artist. Char Jones, and shows history about the origin of nationality. As you can see. the diffeent nationalities made me what I look like today.

AN AFRICAN-AMERICAN MAN

3.0 X 30 Oil Paint On Canvas March 30, 1994
By Charles Jones

This painting represents the artist Charles Jones, some history about the nationality in his genes as for the knowledge that I have within me represents people of color and this is what I look like today those different nationalities made me what I look like today as you can see from this painting.

This painting shows a human being being transformed from a darker color race to a lighter color race. From what I understand about my Great Great Grand Father whom was a former slave made the difference today on what I look like. If a very dark man marries a very light complexioned woman and they have a child most likely the child is going to come out about a medium complexion I was looking on the wall one day at my Great Great Grand Mother picture and I notice that she was not very dark or very black looking person she was about a medium brown complexion, and looked more like a native Indian, so was my grand mother, she was a medium brown complexion, however my mother was a very dark complexion person, which means my grand mother must of had to engage herself with a darker or black man, but when my mother engaged her self with a lighter skin person and from what I hear is that this person was a caucasian person of the Italian race which is what I am trying to represent here on this painting how people of color can create a different type of race with all these different nationalities.

The map of African represents another part of me and the American Flag represents another part of me because American people are of different nationalities even though we are darker or lighter. The heads or faces represents mixing of race, a very dark or black complexion person, a medium complexion person, a very light complexion person or white person and then you have a mixture of one person of how I look today from all the different races carried on by Great Great Grand Mothers and Fathers.

MY DREAM OF DEATH OF ENDLESS DARKNESS

This 30x30 Created January 15, 1994 oil paint represen the artist and his nightmares ofdeath. a vision of endle darkness andlike any living human being, we are going die one day. As you can see, I am standing over myself the painting looking down at my corpse, once a body of li now I lay there cold and stiff, maybe if I am lucky I will buried in a mausoleum, were relaties can see my dead bo somewhat preserved. the skull represents the obvious death, the thought of death like some people may say knowledge of knowing it and probably neverwillo. Death nothing, is probably like a bad sickness of feeling, nothi at all. My vision of death is seeing endless darkness, may some stars, a body, I may vision my corpse, cold as stor all my internal organs completely deteriorating inside me. I no longer exist, only as a memory by others that on knew me.

MATERIAL USED IN THIS PAINTING

Starting with backgound used modeling paste to crea some depth, also used a palette knife to create a spec affect. Allowed to dry and covered with zinc white, cob blue, and naples yellow, for trees used burnt sienna, ra sienna mixed with black. For myself in this painting us cadmium red for sweater and blue black for pants for sk tone used naples yellow, raw sienna and burnt umber, ba cally for the skull used the same as background in sky.

MY DREAM OF DEATH OF ENDLESS DARKNESS

INTRODUCTION GUNS AND VIOLENCE
18X24 OIL - OCTOBER 1, 1993

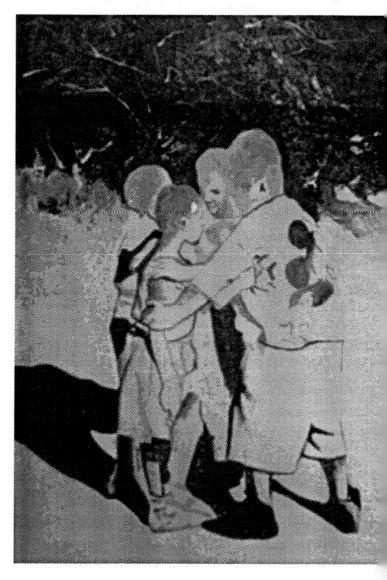

INTRODUCTION GUNS AND VIOLENCE
18X24 OIL OCTOBER 1, 1993 COMPLETE

KILLING OF A TWO YEAR OLD
36x36 OIL PAINT OCTOBER-06-93

The artist recaptured this incident; seen about 20 yeards from were he was at. I heard two shots fired looking out the window; there lay a victim two year old. As i watched the person kneeling over the lifeless body lower his head at the torso, as if to listen for any heart beat at the chest could hear him saying "she's dead". As you can see above the spectator the spirit of the little girl has just left her dead body, meaning her spirit lives on. However, the father of the child was in a mental state of shock and unlimited mental anguish. The family members were outraged.

Another portrait of senseless violence as seen by the artist.

FATHERS
32X46 OIL ON STRETCH CANVAS MARCH 5, 1995

I NAMED THIS PAINTING "FATHERS" BECAUSE FATHERS SEEM TO VANISH, LEAVING A MOTHER, WIFE OR GILRFRIEND AND CHILDREN SUCH A INCONVENIENT SITUATION AS YOU CAN SEE. THE CHILDRN ARE LOOKING FOR AND IN NEED OF HOPE. HOWEVER, IT IS NOT ALWAYS THE FATHERS'S FAULT FOR VANISHSING. IT COULD BE BECUASE OF SOME OTHER UNFORUNATE SITUATION. SO WHY DO FATHERS SUDDENLY DISAPPEAR?

FATHERS
32X46 OIL ON STRETCH CANVAS MARCH 5, 1995

PORTRAIT OF TODAY'S BLACK FAMILIES
March 5, 1995

THE SPECTATOR, GANGS, AND POLICE
39-3/4X48-1/4 OIL, sEPTEMBER 11, 1994

THE PAINTING REPRESENTS TODAY'S GANG VIOLENCE AND POLICE. THE SPECTATOR OBSERVES THE VICTIM BEING UNMERCIFULLY BEATEN WITH PIPES WHILE THE POLICE TRY TO ELIMINATE THE POSSIBILITY OF ANY FATALITIES.

HUSBAND AND WIFE - LATE 1980'S

This painting was done as a restoration. because of the conditoin of the black and white photo, the only thing I had to go on, was the gentleman's head and no torse. So what I decided to do was, use a fashion magazine to sketch a body to the head. After sketching this out, I took both people and brought them together as one. Example you can see what it looks like on a completed canvas; another one of my creative art works - did in a special way.

PLAYERS OF THE CITY 1973
24X30 OIL ON CANVAS

Involving three people man, woman, man; painte
oil.

This painting represents woman and man manipul:
each other, the man is holding a woman who is part
lin and sitting on a chiar, this represents the man
ing on her intellect at the same time lusting for her b
simultaneously, the woman is picking the man's n
his brains protruding from his head, the woman is
ing at it which shows her manipulation. while at
time, two men are putting each other down. She le
one for the other because of ther desires, her fascin:
with his sharp dress andhhis worldiness. Eventuall
or the other will be eliminated.

PLAYERS OF THE CITY 1973
24X30 OIL ON CANVAS

FATHER IN MEMORY OF SON

FATHER IN MEMORY OF SON FATHER WAS ADED TO THIS PORTRAIT TO SHOW THEM BEING TOGETHER, ALWAYS.

FATHER IN MEMORY OF SON
18x23 OIL, OCTOBER 13, 1994

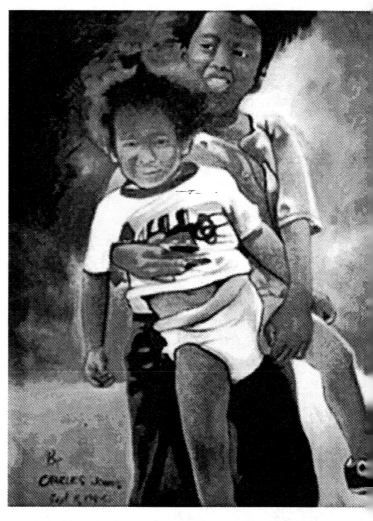

LITTLE GIRL CARRYING BABY BOY
18X24 OIL PAINT, SEPTEMBER 11, 1994

This painting shows two kids enjoying their playful juven years. The girl carrying the small boy, who doesn't wan be carried, but instead would like to run free with restraints.

CHAPTER (6)

SINGLE TITLED PAINTINGS WITH OUT A STORY

If you will notice, only the sinle painting is show there are no stesp as shown on the previous pages

SISTER AND BROTHER PORTRAIT ON A BUTTON
24x24 oil on canvas

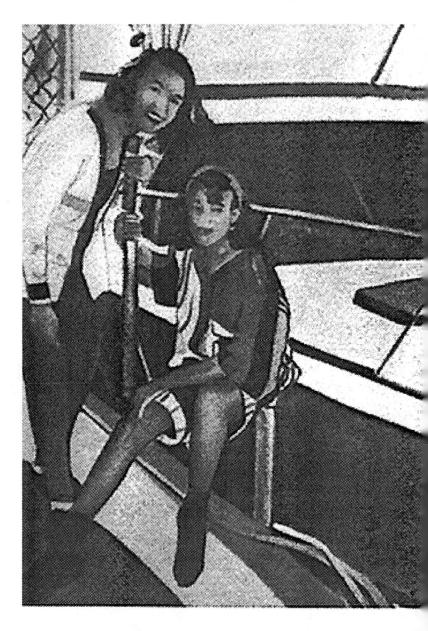

MOTHER AND DAUGHTER ON THE DOCKS

18 x 24 Oil Paint

PORTRAIT OF ARTIST, SON AND NIECE
18X24 OIL

PORTRAIT OF HUSBAND WI
16X20 OIL 12-25-93

A. LAMBERT OF AFFIRMATIVE ACTION
18X24 OIL PAINT

THE ADMIRER OF AFRICAN AMERICAN LEADERS

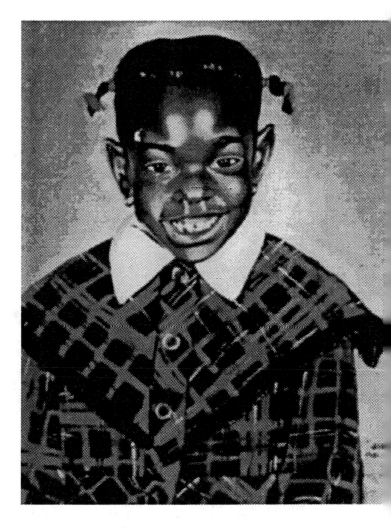

cousin
18x 24 oil paint

PORTRAIT OF YOUNG MAN

PRIMITIVE BOY
18X24 ACRYLIC PAINT ON CANVAS

FIANCE
20X30 OIL PAINT

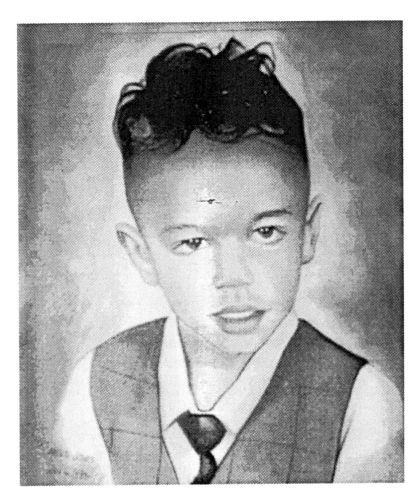

PORTARIT OF BOY
18X24 OIL PAINT, JULY 6, 1994

BROTHER AND WIFE

24X30 OIL PAINT

TAMMIE'S LITTLE BOY
18X23 OIL ON CANVAS 11-09-1994

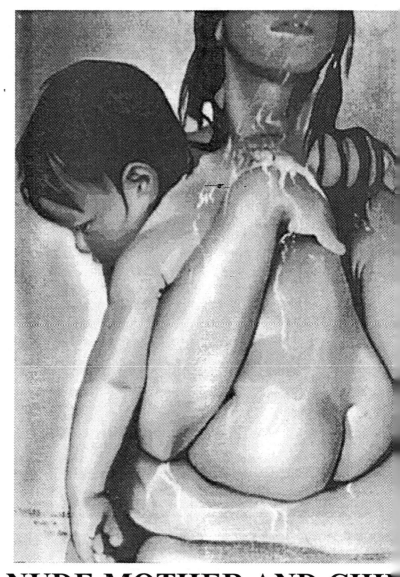

NUDE MOTHER AND CHI[LD]
18X24 OIL

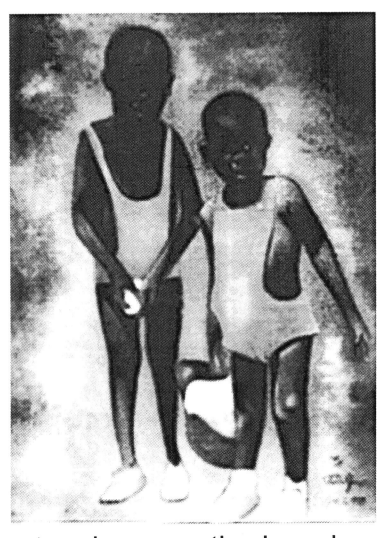

two boys on the beach
18x24 oil

TO MY LOVE
30X34 OIL JUNE 19, 1994

DOUBLE OF M.L.KING
18X24 OIL

LADY DRESSED IN JEWELS
18x24 oil paint

GRANDMOTHER AND AUNT
20x30 oil paint

CURIOSITY OF LITTLE CHILDREN EXAMINING A TRICYCLE

20x 26 OIL ON STRETCH CANVAS
NOVEMBER 1994

SLICK AND SIS
husband and wife oil on canvas

CHAPTER (7)

pictures that were scanned, air brushed and camera taken using a computer

PICTURES THAT WERE SCANNED, AIR BRUSHED AND CAMERA TAKEN USING A COMPUTER

The following pictures were scanned or taken with a computer camera and a computer; I then air brushed using different clolors that were added on the picture or enhanced, such as edited, distored or recreated using your imagination. In order to air brush with a computer you will need a device such as a scanner, a coputer camera and special software that will allow you toadd different colors and sprays in diameters, etc. Adobe photoshop 3.0 will allow you to take advantage of today's technology.

WORKING WITH COMPUTER ART TO HELP YOU WITH YOUR OIL PAINTINGS

NAILS BY SHAI

IN THE CUT
WORKING WITH COMPUTER ART TO HELP YOU WITH YOUR OIL PAINTINGS

NAILS BY SHAI

IN THE CUT
WORKING WITH COMPUTER ART TO HELP YOU WITH YOUR OIL PAINTINGS

MANICURE
PEDICURE
FULL SET
SCULPTURE
SILK WRAPS
HOT OIL

And All Nail Care Services

CAT

By Charles Jones May 25, 1996

THIS PICTURE WAS TAKEN WITH A COMPUTER CAMERA, AND AIR BRUSHED WITH SHADES OF GRAY ARTIST USING HIMSLF AS A MODEL.

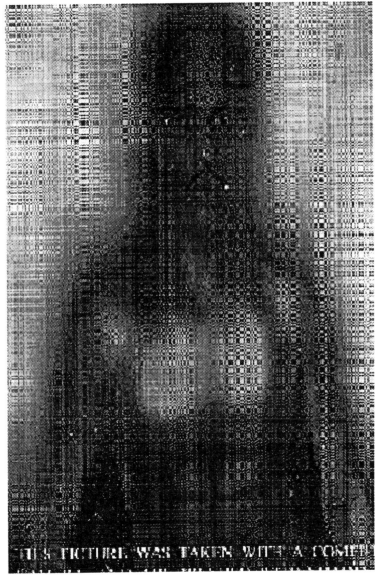

Photos scanned, air brushed, merged with anotheer photograph using a computer and martial art wxample (1)

OIL PAINTING 24X30
This picture was creates using various picutres scanned onto a computer hard drive, to create a cove of martial art book. after this was created from the computer I decided to creatre a painting.

Photoes scanned, air brushed, merged with another photograph using a computer and martial arts example (2)

Photos scanned, air brushed, merged with another photograph using a computer and martial arts example (3)

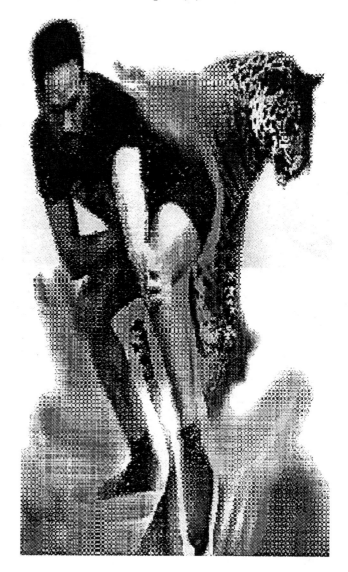

Photos scanned, air brushed, merged with another photgraph using a computer and martial arts example (4)

Photos Scanned, Air Brushed, Merged with another photograph using a computer and Martial Arts Example (5)

Photos Scanned, Air Brushed, Merged with another photograph using a computer and Martial Arts Example (6)

Photos Scanned, Air Brushed, Merged with another photograph using a computer and Martial Arts Example (?)

Photos Scanned. Air Brushed. Merged with another photograph using a computer and Martial Arts Example (8)

Photos Scanned, Air Brushed, Merged with another photograph using a computer and Martial Arts Example #9

Photos Scanned. Air Brushed. Merged with another photograph using a computer and Martial Arts Example (10)

PHOTO SCANNED WITH COMPUTER AND
AIR BRUSHED (1)

WOMAN OBSERVING UNKNOWN ARTIST SKETCH HER IN
CHARCOAL CHALK.
JULY 21, 1996

PORTRAIT OF MODEL AND STATUE
NUMBER (4)
JULY 21, 1990

PORTRAIT OF MODEL AND STATUE
NUMBER (1) JULY 24 1996

PORTRAIT OF MODEL AND STATUE NUMBER (4)
JULY 20, 1996

PORTRAIT OF MODEL AND STATUE
NUMBER 15 JULY 20, 1998

PHOTO SCANNED WITH COMPUTER AND AIR BRUSHED WITH MODEL (5)

NOTES

INDEX

DEDICATION	iii
TABLE OF CONTENTS	iv
PREFACE	v
ACKNOWLEDGEMENTS	vi
INTRODUCTION	1
BRUSHES	2
CHEMICALS	3
PAINTS	4
ART EXHIBITION	5
BOOK SIGNING	6
OPAQUE PROJECTOR	7
CHAPTER (1) ILLUSTRATION AND SETUP	8, 9, 10
EASEL, CANVAS SETUP	11
CHAPTER (2) SINGLE WASH	12, 13
CREATING THE WASH	14
SARAH GARDNER FAMILY	15
TEN YEARS APART	16
INTERMEDIATE FAMILY MEMBERS	17
PORTRAIT OF LISA MCDONALD	18
MOTHER AND DAUGHTER	19
A. LAMBERT	20, 21
MARRIED COUPLE	22
PRIMITIVE INDIAN WOMAN	23
HOMELESS	24
KPORTRAIT OF VERONICA ALEXANDER	25
MARTIAL ART EMBLEM	26
AFRICAN WOMAN MAKING BASKET	27
CHAPTER (3) CREATING A PAINTING	28
CHICAGO LAKE FRONT	29
HOMELESS ON BROADWAY CHICAGO	30
CHAPTER (4) MULTIPLE WASH	31, 32
MICHAEL JORDAN, DUNK SLAM	33, 34
PORTRAIT OF THREE	35, 36
COUSIN & BOYFRIEND	37, 38
GIRL AND BOYFRIEND	39, 40
ARTIST & SON	41, 42
REPEATED VIOLENCE	43, 44
THREE GENERATION OF MOTHER	45, 46
PORTRAIT MOTHER & CHILD	47, 48

INDEX

PORTRAIT GRAY WEDDING	49, 50
C.H.A GROUNDS	51, 52
WOMAN IN WHEEL CHAIR	54, 55
HANDICAPPED & BLIND MAN	57, 58
FANTGASY OF ARTIST BEING KING	60, 61
ARTIST & WOMAN BODY BUILDER	63, 64
CHAPTER (5) ADDING STORES	66, 67
AUTOBIOGRAPHY OF PAINTING	68, 69
MOTHER PULLING BABY BOY	70
MY YOUTH, PAST, UNBORN SON	71
AFRICAN AMERICAN MAN	72, 73
MY DREAMS	74, 75
GUNS & VIOLENCE	76, 77
KILLED TWO YEAR OLD	78
FATHERS	79, 80
SPECTATORS, GANGS POLICE	81
HUSBAND & WIFE	82, 83
PLAYERS OF CITY	84, 85
FATHER IN MEMORY OF SON	86, 87
LITTLE GIRL CARRYING BABY BOY	88
CHAPTER (6) SINGLE TITLE	89
PAINTING WITHOUT STORIES	90
SISTER & BROTHER	91
MOTHER & DAUGHTER ON DOCKS	92
PORTRAIT ARTIST, SON & NIECE	93
WEDDING PORTRAIT OF HUSBAND WIFE	94
A. LAMBURG	95
COUSIN	96
YOUNG MAN	97
OVER WEIGHT GIRL	98
PRIMITIVE BOY	99
FIANCE	100
PORTRAIT OF BOY	101
BROTHER AND WIFE	102
TAMMIE'S LITTLE BOY	103
NUDE MOTHER & CHILD	104
BOYS ON BEACH	105
TO MY LOVE	106
DOUBLE KING	107
LADY DRESSED IN JEWELS	108

INDEX

GRANDMOTHER & AUNT	109
CURIOSITY OF LITTLE CHILDREN	110
SLICK & SIS	111
CHAPTER (7) SCANNED PICTURES	112
WORKING WITH COMPUTER ART	113, 114
FINGER NAILS	115
3D GAL & ARTIST	116
AIR BRUSHED OF ARTIST	117
AIR BRUSHED OF MARTIAL ART	118 to 127
UNKNOWN ARTIST OUT SIDE	128
MODEL WITH STATUE	129, 132
RESPECT OTHERS	133
NOTES	134
INDEX	135 to 137
ORDER FORM	138
COMMENTS	139, 140

ORDER FORM

COMMENTS

COMMENTS

THE AFRICAN AMERICAN ART
OF
CHARLES JONES

SPECIAL COLLECTION
OIL PAINTINGS TO PHOTO
COMPUTER AIR BRUSHED

OVER ONE HUNDRED AND FIFTY PICUTRES
INCLUDED ARE:
ILLUSTRATIONS
OIL PAINTINGS TO COMPUTER AIR BRUSHED
SEQUENCE AND PROCEDURES IN OIL PAINTS
CREATING PAINTINGS FROM A COMPUTER
CREATING PAINTINGS FROM OBSERVING INCIDENTS
CD ROM INCLUDED VIEW ADDITIONAL PAINTINGS
CD ROM TESTED IN WINDOWS98, WINDOWS 2000

U.S. $49.95 ISBN 0-9643501-4
REV: MAY 07, 200